# OUR NATION (NIGERIA) CAN BE GREAT

By

Alex Ndukwe

First printing, 2019

Printed in the United States of America

ISBN: 978-0-359-83168-5

## TABLE OF CONTENTS

## Dedication

This book is dedicated to Pastor E.A. Adeboye, A Father of Nations for his exemplary Leadership qualities.

## Forward

This book has taken me some time to deliver and it is a thing of Joy to see it published today since I began the project in 2017. I want to use this medium to encourage Nigerians that we should not give up on our dear country, let us assume it is a phase that we must undergo to become a great nation.

I need to commend our president for coming up with policies geared at revamping our economy, most recently the closure of our borders that has been a conduit pipe for smuggling goods that are contrabands and having adverse effects on our economy. With an economic team newly inaugurated, reforms are on the way.

Local production of rice which has been in progress and saving us hard earned foreign exchange. Ban on importation of dairy products, textiles etc. are the new reforms that was flagged off recently. Some west African countries have come to learn from us, it's a thing of joy.

The book highlighted our greatest challenge, which is corruption, lack of patriotism. We should not look at personal gains when we have an opportunity to serve our motherland. Nation building is not for government alone, but all hands must be on deck for a greater nation.

Issues that we are witnessing today started from the first republic and it will take some time to correct these problems like infrastructural gap, wasteful spending, neglect of rural areas etc.

We have had predictions that have never come to pass, and this shows that Nigeria is not a mistake but a design by God and no one can destroy with unfounded prophecies from the pit of hell.

Let us come together and support government initiatives, we have no other place even if you have dual citizenship there is no way you can compare foreign lands to Nigeria, Change must begin with every one of us.

Alex Ndukwe

A Patriotic Nigerian

# Introduction

Nigeria, a great country amalgamated in January 1914 by Governor Fredrick Lugard. Over a hundred years after, the country continues to experience decay at all strata & most times discussing Nigeria brings sorrow. Before now, there was a prediction made by the US ambassador to Nigeria, John Campbell in 2011 that Nigeria will not exist beyond 2015. According to him;

***"My view has not changed about the serious challenges Nigeria faces. I think the challenges are more pronounced than they were before the Boko Haram insurrection began in the North. Political life is also unsettled by the approach of the 2015 elections."***

This prediction did not come to pass because there is a seed of greatness in the country and Campbell is a prophet of doom, prayers that are been offered are not in vain. There is no country on earth that has not experienced turbulent times, Nigeria cannot be an exception, reasons why there are such experiences is for us to retrace our steps, eliminate wastes, corruption at all levels, co-exist as one indivisible nation.

In recent time most youths are in the craze of wanting to travel out of Nigeria, this cannot be said to be the solution to the nation's problems but can only compound her woes.

There is still hope for the nation; challenges are bound to be there because of the negative mentality of a large bunch of the populace especially the leaders. Political Leadership is seen as a meal ticket and rather than service to the masses. This can be seen as the reason why you hear of hate speeches across the regions, various associations demanding for secession especially in the South Eastern part of Nigeria. There have been various calls for secession in this part of the country. These calls easily get disgusted that the then leader of Biafra Col. Odemegwu Ojukwu clearly warned that:

***"He said a second civil is not in the best interest of Nigeria, that Nigeria should learn its own lesson***

***and understand that the Igbo always add value to anywhere they go. To any situation they are called upon, they add value. They never go anywhere to deteriorate the existing situation."***

Calling for secession is a selfish agenda and one cannot help but question there can be a consensus candidate for the South eastern part of the country in the event of an election. The role played by the eastern governors in steaming the tide during the Python Dance crisis in 2017 is commendable, even within the so-called Secession agenda, there were still able to hold their ground for Nigeria.

Religious Leaders are not doing much in promoting peaceful co-existence among the citizens. Why there is the experience religious crises is the failure to preach peace and the essence of respecting each other, there is need to emulate the Yoruba tribe, imagine in a family where Muslims and Christians coexist as one family. At this stage in our life as a nation there is need for Nigerians to live together as one despite our religion or ethnicity.

Mr. Peter obi, the former governor of Anambra State made an assertion during Lecture he delivered some time ago in Ebonyi state and he called Nigeria "a failed state", this comment this author believe is unfair. The present challenges of the nation it's a challenge is just a phase, it will be over with time. All the indices not being favourable that does not mean that the trend will continue for ever, a turnaround is in sight. Speaking further, he said:

*"Whenever they talk about Nigeria at 57, I refuse to talk... My opinion is that Nigeria is a failed country, period. And that is why you are seeing so many agitations you are seeing today. The agitation is not ending, it's just beginning...It is a cumulative effect of leadership failure over the several years of this country and you can't stop it because you now have millions of young people in their productive age doing nothing, you can call them anything..."*

This book will among others make suggestions on the issue of unemployment raised the by former governor. The Federal Government of Nigeria made campaign promises of creating 12 million Jobs, the question on every ones lips is the the role of the private sector In creating jobs at the rural areas and empowerment of the youths. There is need to stop blame culture, it is the belief of the author that the country should find a way of the problem.

The accounts and views in this book are balanced and not aimed to attack anyone; it should be regarded as views of a true Nigerian that believes that the great country can return to its status among the comity of nations as giant of Africa. This would definitely happen with improved indices of development. The table below shows..... (ADD WHAT YOU ARE INDICATING WITH THE TABLE)

## Nigerian Economic Outlook (2012 -2016)

| | 2012 | 2013 | 2014 | 2015 | 2016 |
|---|---|---|---|---|---|
| Population (million) | 165 | 169 | 174 | 179 | 184 |
| GDP per capita (USD) | 2,708 | 2,944 | 3,182 | 2,677 | 1,976 |
| GDP (USD bn) | 446 | 498 | 553 | 479 | 363 |
| Economic Growth (GDP, annual variation in %) | 4.2 | 5.5 | 6.2 | 2.8 | -1.6 |
| Consumption (annual variation in %) | 0.0 | 21.1 | 0.6 | 1.5 | - |
| Investment (annual variation in %) | 2.8 | 4.2 | 13.4 | -1.3 | - |
| Industrial Production (annual variation in %) | 1.5 | 0.0 | 5.5 | 0.3 | -5.7 |
| Unemployment Rate | 7.6 | 7.1 | 4.8 | 4.3 | 5.0 |
| Fiscal Balance (% of GDP) | -1.3 | -1.4 | -0.9 | -1.6 | - |
| Public Debt (% of GDP) | 12.5 | 12.6 | 10.6 | 12.1 | 18.6 |
| Money (annual variation in %) | 16.4 | 1.3 | 20.6 | 5.9 | 16.8 |

| | | | | | |
|---|---|---|---|---|---|
| Fiscal Balance (% of GDP) | -1.3 | -1.4 | -0.9 | -1.6 | - |
| Public Debt (% of GDP) | 12.5 | 12.6 | 10.6 | 12.1 | 18.6 |
| Money (annual variation in %) | 16.4 | 1.3 | 20.6 | 5.9 | 16.8 |
| Inflation Rate (CPI, annual variation in %, eop) | 12.0 | 8.0 | 8.0 | 9.6 | 18.6 |
| Inflation Rate (CPI, annual variation in %) | 12.2 | 8.5 | 8.1 | 9.0 | 15.7 |
| Policy Interest Rate (%) | 12.00 | 12.00 | 13.00 | 11.00 | 14.00 |
| Exchange Rate (vs USD) | 156.2 | 160.0 | 183.0 | 199.1 | 304.7 |

| | | | | | |
|---|---|---|---|---|---|
| Exchange Rate (vs USD, aop) | 158.8 | 159.2 | 165.2 | 197.9 | 256.1 |
| Current Account (% of GDP) | 4.2 | 4.0 | 0.2 | -3.2 | 0.8 |
| Current Account Balance (USD bn) | 18.9 | 20.1 | 1.3 | -15.4 | 2.7 |
| Trade Balance (USD billion) | 40.9 | 43.8 | 21.0 | -6.4 | -0.5 |
| Exports (USD billion) | 94.3 | 95.1 | 82.6 | 45.9 | 34.7 |
| Imports (USD billion) | 53.4 | 51.4 | 61.6 | 52.3 | 35.2 |
| Exports (annual variation in %) | -2.9 | 0.8 | -13.2 | -44.4 | -24.4 |
| Imports (annual variation in %) | -14.1 | -3.8 | 19.9 | -15.0 | -32.7 |

| International Reserves (USD) | 44.2 | 43.6 | 34.5 | 29.1 | 25.8 |
|---|---|---|---|---|---|
| External Debt (% of GDP) | 1.5 | 1.8 | 1.8 | 2.2 | 3.1 |

The record NGN 8.6 trillion (approximately USD 28.2 billion) budget focuses on capital spending and targets a deficit of NGN 2.0 trillion, slightly down from the deficit in the 2017 budget. To fund the ambitious spending plans, President Muhammadu Buhari (PMB) stated that the government would borrow over NGN 1.5 trillion, thereby increasing the country's debt burden. While developing badly needed infrastructure could boost economic activity, the government has previously fallen short on revenue and expenditure targets, generating uncertainty as to whether they will meet the 2018 goals. For development to take place there is need to address the decay in the country's infrastructure. The President would have to borrow to upgrade roads, railway tracks, etc.

It is the hope of the author that the various opinions and solutions in this book will be useful in the quest to make Nigeria a great nation as she aims to take her rightful place in the comity of nations.

# Chapter 1

# The Nigerian Economy

Nigerian economy could be described as a mono economy depending sole on the sale of crude oil. The prices often fluctuate and terminologies like excess crude are very common. State governments scramble over these funds. Rather than put these funds for the benefits of their states, they (State Governors) embezzle these into their private pockets there by unleashing untold poverty upon the masses. When the prices of the crude oil crashes, there is an adverse effect on the people. This problem occurs as a result successive governments' refusal to save for such occurrence.

## Precolonial times

Agriculture is a primordial economic activity in Nigeria which formed the means of livelihood of the peoples and a strong factor for the rise of states and empires just as the case everywhere in the world. In the words of Evans

Pritchards "the first evolution that transformed human economy gave man control over his own food supply, man began to plant, cultivate and improve by selection of edible grasses, roots, and trees".

In pre-colonial Nigeria, farmers depended on implements such as digging stick, hoe, cutlass and sickles. The common crops produced based on territorial specialization includes, yam, okra, vegetables, maize, cocoyam, cassava, plantains, bananas, kolanuts and oil palm. Apart from the production of cotton, kolanuts, and palm oil, agriculture in most part of Nigeria was meant food crop production. Food crops produced depended on rainfall, vegetation and types of soil. For an example, in the grassland or savannah north where rainfall is high and for about three to five months in the year – cereals and grains predominated. Sorghum, maize, rice and specially millet were among the most common food crops. In addition, cotton was widely cultivated. In the forest south of Nigeria where rainfall is heavier, root crops such as yam, cocoyam and cassava were widespread. In addition, plantains, bananas, kolanuts, and oil palm also thrived luxuriantly.

The British increased their dominance in Nigeria by securing the oil and ivory trade. She was able to do this by usurping the power of traditional rulers in Nigeria. It was also during this period that the Sokoto Caliphate was formed.The caliphate was in Northern Nigeria as well as parts of neighbouring countries. According to history there were Hausa merchants involved who were in extensive export-trade network and Kano began the commercial capital of the Caliphate as it had the biggest manufacturing centre in the region. The clothing produced in the Caliphate was exported from Kano to various parts of West Africa. Also at this period, the colonial masters controlled every economic activity in all parts of Nigeria at this time. Agriculture was the main occupation; cash crops like cotton, cocoa, groundnut were also produced in commercial quantities.

Nigeria produced 41% of the total groundnut production in West Africa. The groundnut pyramids used to be conspicuous in Kano city of Kano State (northern Nigeria) and proudly pointed out to visitors. The huge piles of sacks that tapered to a point higher than most of the buildings, were a symbol of northern Nigeria's abundance in an important cash crop. Kano was once a staging post in a thriving trade to the market of Europe. Due to the high returns generated, as back as 1912, farmers were encouraged to plant groundnuts and sell to agents buying them at various locations for exportation to Europe.

The oil palm is another Agricultural produce which the colonial masters exploited in the 1900, when the British finally penetrated the hinterland of the Niger Delta, the exploitation of oil palms was paramount in her imperial motives. Of all the principal export commodities during the colonial period, palm oil and palm-kernel have the longest histories being some of the earliest commodities exported from the present-day Nigeria.

The earliest cocoa farms in Nigeria were in Bonny and Calabar in the 1870s but the area proved not suitable for cultivation. In 1880, a cocoa farm was established in Lagos and later, a few more farms were established in Agege and Ota in present day Ogun state. From the farms in Agege and Ota information disseminated to the Yoruba hinterland about cocoa farming, thereafter, planting of the tree expanded in Western Nigeria. Cocoa was the leading agricultural export of the country at that time and Nigeria became the world's fourth largest producer of Cocoa, after Ivory Coast, Indonesia and Ghana.

In 1949,pressure from the professional and commercial elites in Nigeria were propositions in favour of decolonization and independence. As a result of this, the political parties between 1951 and 1960 had begun playing leading roles in unifying and mobilizing the economic elites.

Nigeria became an independent nation in 1960 and fought a bitter civil war that lasted for 3years. The country began enjoying the dividends on crude oil that was discovered a few years before independence.

**Post Independence**

Agriculture took a backstage immediately after the civil war, the black gold became a blessing, and there was prosperity due to the oil boom experienced in the early 1970's. Today, Nigeria is the largest oil producer in sub-Saharan Africa and since 1971 a member of OPEC, with an estimated production volume of 2.413 million barrel/day as at 2005.

By the late 1970s, oil had replaced cocoa, groundnuts and palm products as the country's biggest foreign exchange earner. In 1971 Nigeria was the world's seventh-largest petroleum producer and became a member of the Organization of the Petroleum Exporting Countries (OPEC). The dramatic rise in world oil prices in 1974 caused a sudden flood of wealth that can be described as "dynamic chaos". There was abundance of wealth generated by exports in the crude. This led to wasteful spending and corruption.

Unemployment became an increasingly serious problem. Large numbers of farm workers, who had gone to urban areas in search of higher wages, remained in the cities even if they failed to find jobs, while school graduates and dropouts flooded the labour market at a rate of 600,000 a year in the mid-1970s.

During this time, Gen. Yakubu Gowon's (then Military head of state) regime came under heavy criticism as a result widespread and obvious corruption at every level of national life. Graft, bribery, and nepotism were an integral part of a complex system of patronage and "gift" giving through which influence and authority were asserted.

In 1976, Gowon's regime was overthrown and Gen. Murtala Mohammed's regime was installed to power, what was the economic policy of the Junta one may bother to ask. He swiftly initiated a comprehensive review of the

3rd National Development Plan and created economic strategies to address rising inflation rate. He also immediately announced that his government would encourage the privatisation of government corporations. To fight corruption and over-bloating of the civil service that was legitimised by the Gowon government, he dismissed more than 10,000 public officials and employees without benefits, on account of age, health, incompetence, and or malpractice. A Former minister of petroleum resources in (STATE THE REGIME), Chief Philip Asiodu, says the military fiat with which the Murtala/ Obasanjo regime abandoned the 1975 development plan stifled the growth of the country.

According to him, the 1975 Development Plan was a product of feasibility studies in all sectors of the economy for the purpose of diversification. "This was when Nigeria and the Asian Tigers were at par. Today, we know where the Asian Tigers are and where we are, "he said.

Nigeria had the best opportunities to be a great nation, but the opportunities are been squandered. obviously the nation did not maximize the oil boom that was experienced in 1974.There was no strategy for the way forward, wasteful spending became the order of the day, little wonder the then head of state made an assertion that , **'Money is not our problem, but how to spend it'** , in the opinion of this writer, the military junta plundered the economy, the decay has been revolving from one administration to another. The leaders had no idea of infrastructure apart from roads, schools, hospitals, bridges. Nigeria has lived a life of total waste. In 1977, she hosted the Festival of Black Arts (FESTAC '77), the biggest black festival, what is the purpose? To place Nigeria on the African map as the richest in the continent, just like Mansa Musa of the Mali Empire. Speaking of same matter (ADD THE SPEAKER AND VENUE, OCCASION AND YEAR THE SPEECH WAS MADE) was of the opinion that:

***"...I don't understand the source of the nostalgia. It is provocative. It is pointless. It is insensitive. Is***

***there value in commemorating the anniversary of a cultural festival that was widely adjudged to be wasteful..."***

Eventually came the second republic, the baton was handed over to them as they continued the race of plundering our dear nation in 1979 all in the name of democratic governance while the military watched at the side-lines.

Corruption continued at a very high scale, (ADD FISRT NAME) Dikko, a (ADD HIS POSITION THEN) was involved in many scandals, including the issuance of licenses to imports rice that had risen from 50,000 tons in 1976 to 651,000 tons in 1982 , this is just an example of how the republic was an epitome of corruption at all levels.

Just like usual, the military overthrew the government of shehu Shagari in 1983, and ushered in the Buhari/idiagbon regime. This was the era of war against indiscipline & breaking of warehouses and auction of commodities on the streets. Some politicians were arrested and imprisoned for allegations of corruption. Some of them lost their lives in the process.

# Chapter 2

## Leadership qualities of our Founding fathers

The founding fathers of Nigeria had the interest of their people at heart; they can confidently refer to them as elder statesmen. They fought for the independence of Nigeria and their names and deeds are fondly remembered live in our today.

They had a vision, purpose and an agenda for the people. Corruption and selfishness was not part of them. Someone once described how Prime Minister Tafawa Balewa during his time lived in a village in Bauchi chewing sugar cane with his children, and marvelled at this. This is a sharp contrast to the kind of leaders we have today who cannot do without showing off wealth which could have been stolen from the national coffers.

One of the monsters which menaced the public life of this country up to 14th January, the year 1966 is OPPORTUNISM with its attendant evils of jobbery, venality, corruption, and unabashed self-interest, a truly public-spirited person should accept public office not for what he can get for himself — such as the profit and glamour of office — but for the opportunity which it offers him of serving his people to the best of his ability, by promoting their welfare and happiness. –

A quote from Chief Obafemi Awolowo's letter from prison to Major General John Thomas Aguiyi-Ironsi pressing for his release and that of his colleagues. The letter which was dated March 28, 1966 had the following:

***"...Violence has never been an instrument used by us, as founding fathers of the Nigerian Republic, to solve political problems. In the British tradition, we talked the Colonial Office into accepting our challenges for the demerits and merits of our case for self-government. After six constitutional conferences in 1953, 1954, 1957, 1958, 1959, and 1960, Great Britain conceded to us the right to assert our political independence as from October 1, 1960.***

***Of course, my contemporaries scorned at me, but the facts of history are irrefutable. I consider it most unfortunate that our 'Young Turks' decided to introduce the element of violent revolution into Nigerian politics. No matter how they and our general public might have been provoked by obstinate and perhaps grasping politicians, it is an unwise policy..."***

This aptly captured the thinking of Awolowo and other founding fathers of the country. Although we cannot assert that there was no political violence in the first republic, the ideology of our founding fathers, life style, interest of the people was paramount in their hearts , not what they can get for himself. To buttress the thinking of the then leaders of the country, Chief Obafemi Awolowo in same letter quoted above letter opined that :

***"...Service to humanity was the focus at that time unfortunately was the commencement of the first military junta in our polity..."***

As part of the plans to unify the country towards the move for independence in 1960, there was a coalition government between the Northern People's Congress (NPC) and the National Council of Nigeria and the Cameroons (NCNC), led by Nnamdi Azikiwe. He (Azikiwe) also invited the Action Group (A.G.) to join in the formation of the government. The 1957 cabinet was constituted as an all-party cabinet. Though, Awolowo, the leader of A.G. and premier of the Western region were sceptical of the plan, the national executive committee of Action Group party endorsed the National Government and Ayo Rosiji and Samuel Akintola were nominated by the party. During this period, Alh. Balewa developed a close relationship with K.O. Mbadiwe from NCNC and Samuel Akintola from AG.

Tafawa Balewa formed a national government that brought the political parties together. Azikiwe and Awolowo were all involved and the interest of the nation paramount in their activities.

At this period, one could notice a trace of tribalism in our polity, the regions had their leader and they cannot be described as nationalists, ZIK supported Biafra during the civil war that ravaged south east.

The prime minister, Alh.Tafawa balewa though was presumed to have been appointed by the colonial masters and was protecting their interest, and followed their (colonial Masters) agenda.

**Military in Politics**

The military has been in politics since the coup that removed the first republic. Gen.Aguiyi ironsi came up with reasons of violence, corruption and lack of direction as the reasons for the 1966 coup. Six months later, there was a palace coup. The most senior northern officer was appointed the head of state. Yakubu Gowon from present day Plateau state became the head of state. As at the time of the coup, the economy could be described as been well, exchange rate was 80K to 1 USD. The regime of Gen. Gowon witnessed massive corruption, imported building materials, cement were inflated by government officials.

During this regime, Nigeria witnessed a bitter civil war that lasted for 3 years. By 1970, the then Eastern Region was seriously battered. Nigerians from this region mostly Igbos were denied access to their monies in the bank, the govt only gave 20 pounds to them without taking into consideration what they had in the bank before the war.
In 1973, there was an oil boom, the price of Crude oil was very high in the international market and the country had a fortune from the boom. The government of Gen. Gowon lacked the sense of purpose; they were accused of not knowing how to deploy resources the abundant resources that was at the disposal of the government.

Gen Yakubu Gowon's government was toppled in 1976 by Gen. Murtala Mohammed, 37 year old radical soldier from present day Kano state the government was involved in the fight against corruption that had eaten deep into the fabric of the Nigerian society. The government came up with laudable National Plan that was aimed at diversifying the Nigerian economy. However, Gen. Murtala Mohammed was assassinated within six months of his reign as head of state. This event brought challenges to the Nigerian economy because was still a mono-economy and had the crude oil as its only source of foreign exchange. The crude oil was also having a bad time in the international market.

Gen. Olusegun Obasanjo, the deputy to Gen. Murtala Mohamed assumed duties as the head of state. He started programmes aimed at diversifying the economy. Chief of these programmes was the 'Operation Feed the Nation'; the programme was an attempt to encourage Nigerians to embrace agriculture. The programme did not achieve the desired success as the economy was still struggling.

He (Obasanjo) however successfully returned Nigeria to democracy and the American style of government was adopted. Alh. Shehu Shagari, in 1979 became the president under the flagship of the National Party of Nigeria (NPN), the government of Alh. Shagari otherwise known as the second Republic was known for high scale corruption, a whooping USD 14 billion is believed to have been squandered by the government.

In 1983 the civilian government was toppled by Gen Muhammadu Buhari/Idiagbon, they cited the corruption and lack of direction as the reason for the coup. They came up with "War against Indiscipline", this was aimed at eradicating corruption that was eaten deep into the fabrics of the nation. They arrested all the politicians and imprisoned them, this regime had a very poor foreign policy and they did not receive support from the west. It is wildly believed that Gen. Tunde Idiagbon, the deputy to Gen. Muhammadu Buhari was in charge and was the mouthpiece of the regime. Nigerians during this time lived in fear; press freedom was violated especially with the establishment of Decree 2. Many journalists were imprisoned.

Two years later, Nigerians woke up to martial music on radio, Gen. Ibrahim Babangida had toppled the Buhari/Idiagbon government, they were of the opinion that Nigeria had become a beggar nation and also cited poor economic policy as a reason for the coup. This government lasted for 8 years, the exchange rate nose dived from 80k to =N=4 then to =N=16, the government came up with Structural Adjustment Programme, (SAP), this policy was aimed at cutting down spending. It is noteworthy that Nigeria started borrowing from the International Monetary Fund (IMF), London club, and Paris club during this period and the Naira had to be devalued.

This government experienced a boom in terms of revenue during the gulf war, the proceeds cannot be accounted for, the funds were embezzled by government officers, monies were stashed in swiss banks and other foreign banks. The government also attempted to return Nigeria to civil rule in 1993, the two party-system was adopted. The election was annulled by Gen.

Babangida was under intense pressure to "step aside", he however formed an interim government, headed by Chief Ernest Shonekan. Gen Sani Abacha in a palace coup toppled this interim government and became head of state. His regime ushered in poverty and violation of human rights. Chief of these was the execution of the "Ogoni 9", this group was led by civil rights activist and writer Ken Saro wiwa. The government had what can be described as the worst foreign policy. Prominent Nigerians were thrown into detention and executed secretly. The regime of General Sani Abacha was brought to an end when he died.

Abdulsalam Abubakar became the head of state after Abacha's death in 1998 and returned Nigeria to civil rule.The retired military class lobbied Olusegun Obasanjo to contest for presidency under the flagship of PDP in 1999, this was meant to appease the south-west because of the annulment of June 12 election wildly believed to be won by Chief. Moshood Abiola.

The Military has engaged actively in politics of Nigeria since independence and they have ruled the country for more than 30 years, though some of these juntas had involved technocrats in their government. We cannot downplay the elements of greed and corruption that they claim they want to put things right but end up stealing from the national coffers.

Can the military be really blamed for poor governance? In the opinion of this author, they cannot entirely blamed, the society has experienced moral decadence from the first republic, though looting was not evident at that time , the greatest problem has been that Leadership in our polity since independence lacked vision, sense of purpose and commitment.

There is this assertion that '**a worst military government is better than the best civilian government**', the position of this author is that Nigeria is yet to experience good leadership in Nigeria.

## Politics Today

Good Leadership is what is lacking in Nigeria , the challenge is the style of governance that have been adopted, many are clamouring for restructuring as the way forward , but there is need to deal with some issues that has remained a virus in our system that has deprived us from making progress in our country.

The cost of governance need to be reviewed, it's rather too high and the red and green chamber is the culprit, their allowances are the highest all over the world, many state governors that have finished their tenures scramble for tickets to the red chamber, one reason is because of immunity and the earnings. When will the leaders at different level of governance learn to be servants to the people someone may ask.

In most advance societies, good governance is key to developments experienced in such environments, resignation of political office holders when an issue arise concerning their character is commonplace, their concerns are the people they represent and maintenance of high moral standards.

One cannot help but be thankful for the passing of the #Nottooyoungtorule. The youths have to wake up, they should be prepared to run for public offices, their none involvement in politics have made the old brigade very comfortable.

Nigerians should also remember that they can determine what they want at the polls and outside the polls, The experiences in Sudan, Algeria and other parts of north Africa easily come to mind recently, the people in this countries decided what they wanted and it came to pass, Nigerians has been so docile for too long, we do not need to be violent but embark on peaceful demonstration.

The emergence of the civil society is a good one for the polity; this will ensure there is check and balance in governance. They should be bold enough to speak out when all is not well and come against any form of injustice but should not take laws into their hands.

The National Assembly should as a matter of importance cut their total emoluments by at least 40%, they should understand that they are representing their constituencies; the people voted them into office, their bellies are less important than the people that cut across rural and urban areas in Nigeria. Constituency projects should be evaluated and carried out, the people should not be short changed.

It is good that public officers must declare their assets before assuming duties, corruption that has been a virus in the polity since independence, the war must be sustained, there is need for re-orientation in this direction. Most advanced societies still find traces of corruption, but not at a higher scale like Nigeria's , all hands must be on deck to recover all that have been stolen by public officers.

In advance democracies, the judiciary is independent and not influenced by government in power, they can discharge their duties effectively, this has made such society balanced, and entrenchment of the rule of law. The mockery the judiciary is currently experiencing must stop.

State Governments should look at ways of attracting direct investment from foreign countries to their states. It is a known fact that most states are regarded as not viable; they are unable to pay their bills State leadership should strategize on how their fortunes can improve. The Local Governments (LG) should also look at developing their immediate communities; provide infrastructures that will alleviate poverty and sufferings of the people. Some communities lack portable water, good roads and electricity. It's pertinent to note that rural communities produce the agricultural needs of the country these rural farmers find it difficult to transport their products to the cities, this situation needs to be resolved in other to achieve food security in the country.

The local governments should make efforts to provide infrastructures that will aid food productions, for example mini processing plants that will support the local farmers. These facilities

can be provided and the local governments can earn revenues from it and at the same time alleviate the sufferings of the rural farmers.
Democratic journey of Nigeria started with the first republic, with the shortest life span and now in the third republic have been very stable since 1999 to date. The military have been advised to abstain from politics.

The greatest challenge with Nigeria's democracy is the style of governance and the cost, there is need to streamline it, the era of public office holders appointing various aids should be jettisoned, politicians should not be all out to satisfy friends, party associates that support them financially, morally during electioneering process. This anomaly has over the years affected the quality as well cost of governance in the country.

There is need to reconfigure the senatorial zones, constituencies and reduce the number of law makers. The interest of the nation must be paramount in the hearts of Nigerians, both the rulers and the ruled. Questions need to be asked on the quality of bills passed by the legislature and its importance to nation building. Lawmakers should look at national interest in all their dealings and avoid all form of waste in governance. For Nigeria to take its rightful place in the comity of nations there is need for all hand to be on deck and eliminate waste in governance as much as possible. The electorate are becoming more informed now compared to the past, rigging of elections will be very difficult, the score card of the public office holders determines if they will be re-elected next time and that's the reason why promises should be kept and fulfilled.

The Senate of the Federal Republic of Nigeria (FRN), on Thursday 25 May 2017, passed the Petroleum Industry Governance Bill. The Bill, which still needs to be passed by the House of Representatives and assented to by The President of the before it becomes law, seeks to establish a framework for the creation of commercially-oriented and profit driven petroleum entities, to ensure value addition and internationalisation of the petroleum industry, through the creation of efficient and effective governing institutions with clear and separate roles for the petroleum industry.

The Bill is the first in a series of long-awaited petroleum industry laws designed to reform the Nigerian oil and gas industry. The Petroleum Industry Bill (PIB), an omnibus law meant to regulate the entire sphere of the industry and repeal all current existing oil and gas legislation, had struggled to see the light of day despite its introduction to the National Assembly over 16 years ago.

There is need for the government at all levels to live up to expectation, the standard of living of the masses , maintaining good educational standards, quality health care, Provision of security nationwide , steady power supply, portable drinking water , good road network etc should be at the back of their minds and nothing less than this.

# Chapter 3

## The Enemy Called Black Gold

The crude oil fondly called the black gold was discovered in 1957 at oloiberi in present day Rivers State by shell BP, this discovered crude oil after independence replaced the cash crops that were the only source of foreign exchange. There shift of focus led to decline of Agriculture and forced many people in the rural areas moved to the cities in search of greener pastures.

***The oil boom became a doom because palm produce became unimportant, relatively unimportant to our total economic well-being. We are totally dependent on petroleum. And so***

***efforts to establish plantations and go forward with this crop did not grow.***

The Nigerian economy became dependent on a single product as a source of foreign exchange and revenue. The oil boom experienced in the 1970's led to excess earnings and corruption both in private and public sector. Nigeria experienced the first oil boom in 1973, OPEC had banned exports of crude to the United States this is because (STATE THE REASON), price per barrel rose from 25.97USD to 46.35USD, 2.5 million barrels was produced per day. This is considered to be very lucrative when there is a reaction in the international market.

The oil boom also led to the vocation in the rural area for the urban areas. Before the oil boom, palm oil and other cash crops were the main stay of the Nigerian economy. As a matter of fact, it is wildly believed that Malaysia received their palm oil seedling from Nigeria although this claims is yet to be verified. The earliest record of palm into Far East Asia was four seedlings planted in a botanical garden in 1848 in java in the Dutch East Indies, these seedlings were planted in Malaysia, today they are the largest producers of palm oil in the world which accounts for 44% of world exports. In the 1980s, another important milestone was marked where oleochemicals industry begins to flourish due to ample supply of palm and palm kernel oil. This also led Malaysia to become a world leader in the oleochemicals sector to date.

The entire world is making attempts to embrace green energy, this implies that the dependence on petrol, gasoline will be totally reduced or eliminated.

**Green energy comes from natural sources such as sunlight, wind, rain, tides, plants, algae and geothermal heat. These energy resources are renewable, meaning they're naturally replenished. In contrast, fossil fuels are a finite resource that take millions of years to develop and will continue to diminish with use.**

The number of electric car sales worldwide reached a record high in 2018, with more than 2 million battery electric cars (BEVs) and plug-in hybrids (PHEVs) sold. In the UK alone, data from the Society of Motor Manufacturers and Traders showed a 22% increase in sales compared with 2017.

**Top 10 countries for electric car sales worldwide (2017)**

| **Country** | **New electric car sales*** | **Market share of electric cars** |
|---|---|---|
| China | 579,000 | 2.2% |
| USA | 198,350 | 1.2% |
| Norway | 62,260 | 39.2% |
| Germany | 54,560 | 1.6% |
| Japan | 54,100 | 1.0% |
| UK | 47,250 | 1.7% |
| France | 34,780 | 1.7% |
| Sweden | 20,350 | 6.3% |
| Canada | 16,680 | 1.1% |
| Netherlands | 11,070 | 2.7% |

*Data from the IEA's Global EV Outlook 2018 – *includes BEVs and PHEVs.*

The batteries that power electric vehicles are also improving, says Erik Terjesen, senior strategy director at Massachusetts battery start-up Ionic

Materials. Instead, researchers like him are trying to replace this liquid electrolyte with solid materials such as silicon, to make safer "solid state" batteries that hold more charge.

The advanced countries planned producing electric cars 2 years ago and today the feat have been accomplished and this is definitely a threat to oil exporting countries , the crude will not be in high demand in the future when production of these cars goes fully commercial , the table suggests that the production is in the pilot stage.

In a very short while the market for the black gold will go into extinction, there will be little or no sales in the international market, as technologies point towards green energy and happens to our economy, this remains a very important question to all of us and we must be proactive, developing sectors like agriculture, explore mineral resources in commercial quantities for export.

Among the many frustrations in development, perhaps none looms larger than the "**resource curse**." Perversely, the worst development outcomes--measured in poverty, inequality, and deprivation--are often found in those countries with the greatest natural resource

| | EXPORTED NIGERIAN CRUDE OIL, 2017 | |
|---|---|---|
| **SN** | **COUNTRY** | **QTY(BARRELS) MILLION** |
| 1 | INDIA | 131 |
| 2 | USA | 94 |
| 3 | SPAIN | 66 |
| 4 | SOUTH AFRICA | 36.12 |
| 5 | TOGO | 15 |
| 6 | COTE D'IVORIE | 10 |
| 7 | BRAZIL | 7 |
| 8 | ARGENTINA | 5.96 |
| 9 | URUGUAY | 3.77 |
| 10 | INDONESIA | 24 |
| 11 | CHINA | 5.77 |
| 12 | CANADA | 24 |
| 13 | NETHERLAND | 59 |
| 14 | FRANCE | 46 |
| | SOURCE: NNPC | |

endowments. Rather than contributing to freedom, broadly shared growth, and social peace, rich deposits of oil and minerals have often brought tyranny, misery, and insecurity to these nations

These were the exports done in 2017; the second largest buyer the United States stopped buying Nigeria's crude in 2018. There is no conspiracy for the U.S. not to buy oil from Nigeria.

Price of oil is determined by international market and business people go to get the best product for the best price. That something happened to us with oil. Although the immediate past minister of state for petroleum kachikwu promised that U.S. will resume the purchase of the crude soon.

There are indications that the sales of crude will drop as U.S. will buy limited quantities of our crude, this shows that there will be a decline of sales and more so innovations in green energy in the advanced countries will be a major factor, heavy investments have been made in developing electric cars, solar power farms to power manufacturing firms in Europe and America.

What happened to other mineral resources in the country. The author quite agree that the government had established agencies to ensure that can exploit these

resources and probably export in the nearest future. These agencies impact(s) is yet to be felt. Many mineral resources are found in Nigeria and some of them and their locations nationwide are:

| SN | MINERAL | LOCATIONS WHERE IT'S FOUND | QTY |
|---|---|---|---|
| 1 | BARITES | BENUE,CROSS RIVER,ADAMAWA,YOBE,NASSARAWA, ENUGU, TARABA | 2,000,000 MT |
| 2 | BENTONITE | YOBE,ABIA,ANAMBRA,ADAMAWA,EDO,IMO, EBONYI,AKWA IBOM,CROSS RIVER,BENUE,BORNO | 1,200,000MT |
| 3 | COLUMBITE | PLATEAU,KANO,KADUNA,BAUCHI,KOGI, KWARA,NASARAWA | NA |
| 4 | CASSITERITE | PLATAEU,BAUCHI,KANO,CROSS RIVER,EKITI,KADUNA,NASSARAWA | 300,000MT |
| 5 | COAL | BENUE,ENUGU,NASARAWA,GOMBE,EDO ,ANAMBRA,ABIA,ONDO | 500,000,000MT |
| 6 | MARBLE | OYO,EDO,NASARAWA,KOGI,KATSINA,NIGER,FCT | 80,292,000MT |
| 7 | GOLD | CROSS RIVER,EDO,KADUNA,KATSINA,KEBBI,NIGER,OSUN,ZAMFARA | NA |
| 8 | GYPSUM | ADAMAWA,TARABA,BENUE,GOMBE,OGUN,IMO,BORNO | 2,000,000MT |
| 9 | IRON ORE | KOGI,NASARAWA | 478,000,000MT |
| 10 | GEMSTONE | PLATEAU,BAUCHI,YOBE,BORNO,OGUN,ONDO,KWARA,KOGI,IMO | NA |
| 11 | KAOLIN | KATSINA,PLATEAU,OGUN,BAUCHI,EKITI, ONDO,ANAMBRA | 3,600,000MT |
| 12 | LEAD/ZINC | NASSARAWA,PLATEAU,TARABA,BAUCHI ,GOMBE,EBONYI,IMO,KANO,BENUE | 20,000MT |
| 13 | TANTALITE | NASARAWA,KADUNA,KWARA,KOGI | NA |
| 14 | LIMESTONE | ENUGU,CROSS RIVER,OGUN,EDO,BENUE,GOMBE,SOKOTO,ADAMAWA,EBONYI,IMO,YOBE | 1,355,980,000MT |
| 15 | TALC | NIGER,OSUN,KWARA,KOGI,KADUNA,FCT | 40,000MT |
| 16 | GRANITE | PLATEAU,ONDO,OGUN,BAUCHI,BORNO, ADAMAWA,KOGI,CROSS RIVER,BENUE,OYO,IMO | 3,000,000MT |
| 17 | SALT | NASARAWA,TARABA,ENUGU,CROSS RIVER,BENUE,EBONYI | NA |

There are still other minerals not in this table like – clay, bitumen, phosphate, mica, silicon sand, rutile, kyanite, manganese, fluorite, trona, marble are among the ones not found in the table.

Agriculture scientist in the country needs to come up with innovations that will boost Nigeria's self-sufficiency, think ways of developing storage facilities and other innovations. Policies should be rolled out by government to encourage food production and the Central Bank of Nigeria (CBN) should extend the anchor borrows programme for other food production like poultry, animal husbandry and other Agro allied ventures that will boost food production.

The Federal Government as well as the State and Local governments should remain active in this area and encourage the Argic venture to the fullest. At the local government level, allocations been sent directly from FAAC (WRITE THE FULL MEANING) to the local governments within framework from NFIU (STATE THE FULL MEANING) to ensure accountability of these resources, the local governments should invest in Agricultural infrastructures such as rice mills, palm oil mills, Garri processing machines and other agro allied processing mills that will alleviate the pains of our local farmers and make food production a reality and generate revenues for the local councils. Limitations in processing rice should be addressed; this will help in making them efficient and prices of these commodities reduced.

The private sector should not be left out, they should also participate in this laudable idea to make our nation great in food production and enable us to feed the entire world.

There is need to stop empowerment just for election purposes and other sundry purposes instead of giving the citizens a real economic boast. For an example, during the run off to the 2019 election, Borno state government in a bid to gain electorates support, "empowered " 5000 youths with shoe shining business kits (So-bata). This gesture caused a lot of uproar in the polity. The action was heavily criticized by many.

In another unfortunate incident, Abba Anwar, the Chief Press Secretary to Abdullahi Ganduje, Governor of Kano State, said that the state government would pay N30million as dowry for 1,500 brides during a mass wedding scheduled to hold in the state.

Anwar in the statement said that the government has concluded arrangements to conduct mass wedding for 1,500 prospective couples across the 44 Local Government Areas of the state. The sum of N20,000 would be given by the state government as dowry for every bride, amounting to N30million.Looking at this piece of information, one cannot help but feel sad. It is quite agreeable that Kano state government want to ensure they fix a societal problem but should they as a government not think, once more not think about "how to want to provide Fish" rather than "teaching them how to fish". Thirty million Naira would have been deployed in a better program than conducting a wedding and putting the couples into abject poverty, it should be noted that the marriage will produce children, how the children will be taken care of is a question yet to be answered. When will the government learn to empower the people correctly? As if this is not enough, a similar incident happened in Imo State when the State government created the "Ministry of Happiness and purpose Fulfilment". In the words of the government's spokesperson,

***"..I say this with every sense of responsibility in the understanding that Section 14, subsection 2 of the 1999 constitution makes the welfare and security of the people, the cardinal objective of government...So, what the Governor of Imo State has done in creating the ministry of happiness***

***and purpose fulfilment is to be able to assist Imo people to realise happiness which is the primary essence of government....and their purpose in life".***

It is rather unfortunate that government has lost ideas and creating a conduit pipe for embezzlement of public funds. Creating ministry of happiness so as to ensure that the people will realize happiness is rather a white elephant project. Good governance should give the people been governed happiness when issues pertaining to unemployment is addressed, economy improves , salaries of public servants is paid on time etc. , on the other hand the vulnerable in the society are empowered.

Evidence from Positive Youth Development programs show that if young people have adequate knowledge, skills, and support, sector specific outcomes will improve. Improved outcomes may include quality of health, school and economic success, as well as meaningful contribution and engagement within

Communities.

# Chapter 4

## Education in Nigeria

Nigeria educational system has undergone series of decay over the years as a result of poor funding, if you take a critical look at the budget made yearly by various governments over the years, you will discover that allocations made towards this sector is usually the least.

According to publication by the Centre for Social Justice titled: "Right to Education in Nigeria" the financial projections that were made for capital projects in Vision 20:2020 and the education sector budgets 2009-2013 showed a gross disconnect, as it recorded a shortfall of over N346.8billion.

Similarly, a review of the fiscal projections of the transformation agenda and education sector budgets also reveals a shortfall of N28.7 billion. Furthermore, the financial provisions in the transformation agenda and the SURE-P made provision for vocational education and implementation so far, has not been encouraging.

An analysis of the budgetary provisions for the year 2009-2013 showed that the budget was suffused with recurrent expenditure while capital expenditure received an average of 18.1%. This is below expectations in the Educational sector for all fast track initiative benchmark of at least 20% of the sector budget being allocated to capital projects. On the average, over the 2009-2013 periods, only 55.4% of the total released capital budget for the sector was utilized for major projects. This shows low absorptive capacity on the part of the federal ministry of education. Further, the average utilization rate vis-à-vis the overall education capital budget was 44.7% over the period. The percentage of capital budget released on the average was 60.15% and the percentage of capital budget cash backed amounted to 57.22%. Looking at all this, we can say that Nigeria did not meet the 26% budget benchmark set by UNESCO for education funding.

Nigeria does herself a great harm to herself as a nation by not providing adequate funds to this critical sector. The poor execution of the funds provided has led to non-provision of required infrastructures, standards fallen drastically to the point that the nations graduates cannot be trusted to deliver what they studied in school. The system has so decayed to the extent that parents collaborate with school administrators to indulge in examination malpractices. This development has a grievous effect on both the long and short term development of the nation.

***" Revitalisation is central to our academic work. Unless that area is addressed, our members will still have issues. We are not demanding for N50 billion, we are saying that the minimum that FG can release to reactivate revitalisation fund is N50 billion".***

*{'ASUU strike continues as lecturers meeting with FG ends without agreement', January 21,2019 , Azeezat Adedigba , Premium times}*

Incessant strikes actions have over the years been a reoccurring decimal in the nation's education sector. The unions, led by the Academic Staff Union of Universities (ASUU) has embarked on strike actions countless times with the latest coming on November 4 2018. The strike was embarked over the poor funding of Nigerian universities and non-implementation of previous agreements by the government. These strikes by ASUU has become a common phenomenon in the tertiary institutions and one valid question is that must the academic trade unions always go on strike before the government will do the needful? These disruptions affect students academic pursuit negatively especially on their expected year of graduation. The leaders must be seen as living up to expectation in giving the education sector the attention it deserves.

According to agreement between ASUU and the Federal Government, it stipulates that public universities need N1.3 trillion for a modest revitalisation. The fund was to be released in tranches of N200 billion in 2013, N220 billion 2014, N220 billion 2015, N220 billion in 2016, N220 billion in 2017 and N220 billion in 2018. The previous government of Dr. Goodluck Jonathan was said to have released N200 billion in 2013. But since then, nothing has been released.

ASUU cannot be entirely blamed for the issues popping up in the educational sector. Nigerian public tertiary institutions' standards have in recent times not been doing well in world rankings. ASSU's aim is to improve on the competitiveness of Nigerian graduates. This can be achieved only through improved funding of the institutions. There is an improvement with respect to the ranking of Nigerian universities. Three Nigerian institutions featured in the 2019 Times Higher Education World University Rankings. They include;

1. Covenant University.
2. University of Ibadan
3. University of Nigeria, Nsukka.

This is a slight improvement for Nigeria, compared to last year's ranking where only one school, the University of Ibadan, made the list and was ranked 801–1000.No Nigerian university is ranked among the first 100, 3 schools made the list and from my assessment, this is a poor performance, let's look at statistics released by NUC. According to the National Universities Commission (NUC), Nigeria presently has 43 Federal Universities, 48 State Universities, and 79 Private Universities.

This implies that there are 170 universities in Nigeria, 3 out of 170 means that only 1.76% of the institutions are recognized. We need to step up our standards with respect to all our schools in Nigeria, The Governor of Kaduna state litmus test was highly criticized, but rather we should commend their efforts. How can a teacher lecture children when you cannot pass simple maths exam, then what will such teacher teach in this jet age.

Education has a great social importance especially in the modern, complex industrialized societies. Philosophers of all periods, beginning with ancient stages, devoted to it a great deal of attention. Accordingly, various theories regarding its nature and objective have come into being.

There are enough universities in the country and the National Universities Commission should stop approving new ones, focus should be on to equipped the already existing federal universities, the regulators should also ensure the private and state universities maintain good standards.

**Government Secondary School, Jos, Plateau State**

With every of sense of urgency, the Federal Ministry of Education must now initiate an operation to radically give the nation's Unity Schools a massive facelift, as a place of educational formation and basic capacity development. Although there is an influx of private secondary schools, the public schools have lost its glory, the ministry of education should ensure standards are maintained, high school fees do not guarantee good educational standards.

The ministry of Education budget for 2018 reads, "Rehabilitation of classrooms, laboratories and hostels in Federal Unity Colleges – N573,389,940; Rehabilitation and equipping of laboratories in 104 Federal Unity Colleges – N473,389,940; Continuation of inauguration and follow-up action of reform desk officers in all the parastatals and in the 104 Federal colleges – N1,593,341; "Monitoring and evaluation of technology and science education projects (Science laboratories, vocational enterprise institutions and development partners)

N11,312,718; organising science, technology, engineering and mathematics for 500 students nationwide to increase female enrolment and quality – N19,241,931; capacity building of 500 science, technical, vocational, mathematics, information and communication technology for teachers on usage of modern equipment in schools – N47,319,930.This is a good step in the right direction and should not end here, the execution of this plan is very important so as to ensure the past glories return immediately, if you ask me it's a conservative budget by federal ministry of education.

As a nation, high educational standards will not only mean that the children will receive quality education only but it also has a positive effect on the society , it's a right direction by making the country become great in all ramifications , bringing up great minds would ensure developments cannot be compromised.

# Chapter 5

## Individuals' Role in Nation building

Most citizens of a nation keep blaming government for poor performance. This is a common trend all over the world and Nigeria is not an exception.

I would like to ask a simple question, what's your role as an individual in nation building, your valid contributions are very essential in this direction, one of the greatest problem is the thin finance at the disposal of most governments around the world, borrowing all the time will mortgage the future of generations yet unborn.

In Nigeria, however, there are some people who represent her national importance by calling her the 'Giant of Africa'. This is an inscriptive perspective. Nigeria is called the giant of Africa not necessarily because of the quality of her national institutions and values, but simply by virtue of her large population and oil wealth. The greatness of a nation must be earned and is not determined just by the size of its population or the abundance of its natural resources.

It is important to look at the evolution of theories of nation-building and at the other concepts which it has both supplanted and included. Many people believe that nation-building is evolutionary rather than revolutionary; that is takes a long time and is a social process that cannot be jump-started from outside. The evolution of the Italian city-states into a nation, the German city-states into the Zollverein customs union and later a nation, the multiple languages and cultural groups in France into the nation of France, the development of China from the warring kingdoms, took a very long time, and were the result, not only of political leadership, but of changes in technology and economic processes (the agricultural and then industrial revolutions), as well as communication, culture and civil society, and many other factors.

The first major question that needs to be asked is whether nation-building should be done at all. In the context of intractable conflict, is nation-building an appropriate method of providing stable peace and a secure community, which can meet the needs of the people within it? There are mixed conclusions here. The democratic peace hypothesis argues that democratic states do not initiate wars, or alternatively, in its more limited version, do not initiate wars against each other. Nigeria faces five main nation-building challenges:

(1) The challenge from her history

(2) The challenge of socio-economic inequalities

(3)The challenges of an appropriate constitutional settlement

(4) The challenges of building institutions for democracy and development

(5) The challenge of leadership. In our quest for nation-building, we have recorded some successes, such as keeping the country together in the face of many challenges.

These challenges continue to keep the country from achieving her full potential.

There is need to look beyond current challenges facing the country, the focus should be how they can be overcome and how to stop its negative impact on the progress of the nation. Nigeria is faced with numerous vices and some of them includes:

Corruption
Insecurity
Poverty
Poor Leadership
Violence during elections
Neglect of rural areas
Food insecurity
Mismanagement of infrastructure

**Corruption** – what's the most effective way of fighting corruption, it should start with everyone. Every Nigeria should not engage or encourage it as much as possible. This role is very important. Role in this is very important. In offices, nobody should engage in stealing with pen, it comes in various dimensions; over invoicing, diversions of public funds, embezzlement of public funds, inflation of figures e.t.c. one might ask questions like "what if I'm a subordinate what should I do?", politely refuse to be used and advise your boss to desist from this act, if it falls on deaf ears blow the whistle and the appropriate agencies will take it up from there. Let's think of our nation first and the effect it will have on us as a people.

Religious leaders have a pivotal role to play in this regard, the need to devote time to teach their followers on the dangers of corruption and the importance of putting the nation first against any selfish interest.

**Insecurity** – Nigeria is currently faced with numerous security challenges. Activities of armed robbers, bandits, kidnappers, terrorists and others have made the country unsafe for the citizens. This security challenge has for some time posed a serious challenge to successive governments. Nigerians should get themselves in the fight against insecurity by given out information to security operatives and monitor for any unusual activities around their vicinity. During Boko Haram attacks in Kano State some years back, whenever a strange person noticed in an area, the security agents is informed, arrests are made when necessary.

Security is a collective responsibility; we are all stakeholders in our immediate environments. When there is no security it affects us as a nation, foreign investors will refuse to come and invest in our economy.

We cannot actualize our potentials as a Nation. Everybody should cooperate with the security operatives to make the society secured for everybody. Leaders in communities should not aid and protect these criminals, rather they should expose them.

**Poverty** – Without mincing words, the government and Non Governmental Organisations are playing very important role in this regard, as an individual what are doing to complement their efforts is a question we need ask ourselves. As a professional how can you touch lives with your little earnings, there's a lot that can be done, it's pertinent for us to identify where we can render such supports, for example motherless baby homes, IDP camps, rural communities etc. You can put smiles on the faces of these people; probably periodically you can distribute food items, educational materials at these places.

**Poor Leadership** – Nigeria's population is estimated to be over 200 million with the youths said to be more than 50% of the number. These youths has the ability to determine what happens during and after the electoral process. Rather than do these, they are more concerned about social media and what happens there. Most youths do not play active roles in the elections and that development is worrisome in the development of Nigeria. The society is pointing towards this direction. A revolution does not need the shedding of innocent blood; rather the power of our PVC will affect the change that we desire. The political class will have no choice but to govern well and meet the expectation of people. Your role is to be involved in the electoral process rather than complaining about bad leadership all the time. With a good leader we will place our country on a solid foundation that will make our country sure footed. Becoming an agent of change should be the focus and this should be sorted out on Election Day.

**Violence during election** – Election violence should be avoided during electioneering process, no matter how much you are offered, none of these people are greater than Nigeria. Election violence does no one any good rather it brings up unqualified leaders and below par representations when "elected". The citizens, especially the youths should avoid electoral violence as it jeopardises the system.

**Neglect of rural Area** - Interestingly most people belong to a rural area, only a few can describe their communities as cities. As a professional in any field, Community service should be offered in any capacity to the people. Effects should be made to improve on the lives of the rural dwellers. Well to do people should make it a priority to "give back" to their local communities.

Community developmental projects like building of schools, roads, hospitals as well as award of scholarships to indigent students should be embarked on periodically in these rural areas.

**Food insecurity** – We have stressed so much on agriculture in this book, I will want to advise every professional to engage in subsistence farming, I'm already considering this too, my wife had gone to Nasarawa to negotiate for a piece of land and the labourers that will till the land for me. What if everyone engages in this, what's your view, operation feed your self comes alive and you will reduce some cost that would have been incurred. For some of us that live in large compounds, we can utilize the small space and plant yam, create an artificial fishponds etc, if 40% of our population should do this can you imagine what the definition of food security will be.

**Mismanagement of Infrastructure** - Government invests heavily providing infrastructure, citizens has a role to play by ensuring they are not vandalised. People should be on the look out to make sure these infrastructures are not stolen or vandalised. As a citizen of the country, it is a civic responsibility to protect the properties of the country. The era of people having a nonchalant attitude toward government properties should be discarded and a more patriotic attitude toward adopted. Any action taking in this regard is a step in the right direction in nation building.

# Chapter 6

## What's our direction now?

The title of this chapter is a question for every Nigerian out there. Most advanced societies in world had passed through more turbulent times and horrifying Experience, but one can say that Nigeria cannot afford to lose hope now.

Over the past 30 years, Vietnam for an example has had a remarkable development record. Economic and political reforms under Đổi Mới, launched in 1986, he has spurred a rapid economic growth and development and transformed Vietnam from one of the world's poorest nations to a lower middle-income country.

On the other hand, Sweden has a gross domestic product (GDP) per capita income of $52,311, which is among the highest in the EU. It has low inflation and a healthy banking system. This has not always been the case. Historically, the Swedish economy suffered from low growth and high inflation, the Swedish krona (Swedish currency) was repeatedly devalued. Sweden was also hit by a severe financial crisis in the early 1990s, Banks were unstable and two had to be nationalised, unemployment rose sharply, government spending soared, as did national debt.

The path back to stability and success was not easy for Sweden. But by pursuing inventive and courageous reforms – and sticking to them – Sweden has transformed its economy, paving the way for robust growth in the face of global economic uncertainty.

Vietnam and Sweden faced economic crises in 1986 and 1990 respectively. Their respective governments had to embark on political & economic reforms, today they experiencing a pleasant economy. They both made reforms and they stood by them. We need to stop deceiving ourselves, there is a need to urgently review cost of governance, as mentioned earlier, the lawmakers are overpaid, their earnings should be reduced by 40%, Life pensions for past public office holder should be reviewed, basically this might not solve our problems, this advice is because of moral reasons.

As a nation we reel out action plans and we don't handle them strictly, we will remind ourselves once more, let's itemize them;

**National Development Plan: 1962-1968**

This much said plan was designed as a coordinated effort between the federal and regional governments with emphasis on technical education, agriculture and industry; it also allowed a mixed economic system. About 15% of GDP would be invested and a 4% GDP growth rate was envisioned, this number mildly differed with the 3.9% from 1952-1962.

The Kainji dam construction and the development of the lower Niger River was described as the cornerstone of the plan, other projects included the construction of a 125,000 ton iron and steel mill, An oil refinery,

Construction of 2,000 miles of farm to market road and extending the Northern Nigeria railways by about 293 miles. The plan also made loans available to regional governments to pass on as credit to farmers or for agricultural related projects.

In the West, in terms of agricultural development, the Akintola led government initiated a tree to crop system to spur cash crop productivity with the use of fertilizers. Both the East and Western governments later established farm settlements as part of the development project. The development plan was seen by some has lacking enough feasibility studies prior to implementation. Also, the high dependence on foreign aid exposes the country to conditional assistance whereby the assisting countries may decide to tailor aid to specific areas. The formulation of the plan also involved foreigners, considering the country had just received independence, the move may have led to a mistrust of the plan's intended benefit, the country or developed nations.

## SECOND NATIONAL DEVELOPMENT PLAN (1970-74)

The second National Development was launched shortly after the end of the civil war as a means of reconstructing the facilities damaged by the war and promoting economic and social development throughout the nation. The plan aimed at a capital expenditure programme of N3, 192 Billion during the four years and this was expected to be distributed between the public and the private sectors. The public investment programme was set at N2, 100million while the private sector was expected to make an investment of N1, 632 billion.

The implementation of this capital programme was expected to result in a rise in the gross output of the economy from a level of N3, 028 billion in 1969-70 to N3, 987 billion in 1973 in real term. The average growth rate expected throughout the plan period was about 7 percent per annum.

Five objectives or goals were set for the plan to establish Nigeria firmly, they are:

1. A just and egalitarian society
2. A land of bright and opportunity for the Citizens.
3. A great and dynamic economy.
4. A free and democratic society and
5. A just and self-reliant nation.

There were some achievement in the second national plan, most manufacturing establishments were fully reactivated in this plan; for instance the Calabar and Nkalagu cement factories were not only brought back into production. The second oil refinery was implemented at Warri, the super phosphate Fertilizer project came into being at Kaduna.

In the educational sector, a remarkable achievement was recorded, for example the primary level enrolment raised from 3.5 million in 1970 to about 4.5 million in 1973. At the secondary level, the number of students almost doubled from about 343,300 in 1970-71 to approximately 649,990 in 1973-74.

In the transport sector, about 2,200 miles of roads ware reconstructed. There was the construction of Kano, Lagos, Jos, Morin and Calabar airports. The National shipping line bought two new ships during the second plan period to replaced expensive chartered vessels, while the Nigeria Airways acquired two Boeing 707, two Boeing 737 and two-F-28 aircraft during the plan period.

In the Agricultural sector, most of the farms and plantations abandoned during the civil war particularly in the Eastern states were rehabilitated and bought back into production. Due to the role and importance of agriculture in the Nation's economy, the government intensified the provision of fertilizers and other requirements to farmers during the plan period, Irrigation facilities were provided and Dams were constructed.

## FAILURE OF THE PLAN

Nigeria had substantial deficits on current account in the balance of payment for the first three years of the plan period. These deficits raised quire rapidly, from N50 million in 1970 to 219 million and N317.6 million in 1972.

The plan strategy did not resolve the basic factor problems of Nigeria, rather the planner's claimed that the most serious bottleneck (problems) was the problem of foreign exchange availability required to import machinery and raw materials. Pacts in the development plan did not show any initiative as regards the evolvement of an indigenous technological base. This is because the country has developed strong and ambivalence" attitudes towards foreign investments, foreign technology and technical know-how. This does not augur well for a meaningful economic development.

## Third National Development Plan, 1975-1980

The most ambitious plan which Nigeria has ever launched. Whilst the first national development plan involved a capital expenditure of N2.2. billion and the second national development plan an expenditure of N3.0 billion, the Third National Development Plan proposed a capital expenditure of N30.0 billion, which was later increate to N43.3 billion as a result of oil boom.

Serious concern for rural development at the national level was first highlight in the third nationally radical package towards rural infrastructural development. The objectives of the plan are similar to those of the second national development plan. The plan emphasized the need to reduce regional disparities in order to foster national unity through the adoption of integrated rural development.

The plan provided for rural electrification scheme, the establishment of River Basin Development Authorities (RBDAs), The construction of small dams and boreholes for rural water supply, the clearing of feeder roads for the evacuation of agricultural produce and the supply of electricity to rural areas from large irrigation Dams. At the State Level, some governments like Oyo State showed their intention to transform the rural areas through the provision of basic infrastructural facilities.

The third plan originally projected a capital expenditure of N30.0 billion and was revised upwards to N43.3 billion in 1976 due to the massive increase in oil revenue without any evidence of a new absorption capacity to support such flamboyance. Despite the plan's goal of improving living conditions of the rural people, the resource allocation pattern was even more urban-based than the previous plans. In fact, the aided and abetted the resultant massive rural-urban migration. The plan also failed to recognize the key employment – generating role of the small-scale industries.

Like other plans before it, the third plan did not really achieve its set targets. Irrespective of the inadequacies of this plan, it witnessed achievements in some areas.

**Fourth National Development Plan. (1981-85)**

The fourth national development plan was launched in 1981 to cover the period 1981-85. It was intended to further the process of establishing a solid base for the long-term economic and social development of Nigeria. Emphasis was consequently placed on key sectors such as agriculture, manufacturing, education, manpower development and infrastructural facilities.

Secondly, the plan was considerably bigger than the past ones with a projected Capital expenditure of about N82 billion. Also it was the first plan in which the local government participated following their constitutional position as a distinct level of government with specific responsibilities. The specific objectives set for the fourth plan period were as follows;

i. Increase in the real income of the average citizen.

ii. More even distribution of income among individuals and socio-economic groups.
iii. Reduction in the level of unemployment and under employment.
iv. Increase the supply of skilled manpower.
v. Reduction of the dependence of the economy on a narrow range of activities.
vi. Balance development; that is the achievement of a balance in the development of the different sectors of the economy and the various geographical areas of the country.
vii. Increased participation by citizens in the ownership and management of productive enterprises.
viii. Greater self-reliance, that is, increased dependence on local resources in seeking to achieve the various objectives of the society.
ix. Development of technology

x. Increase in productivity

xi. The promotion of a new national orientation conductive to greater discipline, better attitude to work and cleaner environment.

## Failure of Plan

No sooner was the plan (WHICH PLAN?) launched in 1981, and then the world oil market weakened. By 1983, the level of Nigeria's oil dropped substantially from 2.1millon barrels per day in February 1983. The plan therefore had to be reviewed in 1984 in view of the sharp decline in the resources available for its implementation. The performance of the economy during the fourth plan period was however generally poor; various projects which had been stated for execution during the period were in most cases under funded as a result of the financial crisis resulting from development in the other sectors of the economy had predicted.

The fifth national development plan (2008-2011)

The plan was to come up with 7 points agenda and they are as follows:

Power and energy - The plan is to develop an adequate power supply to ensure Nigeria's ability to develop as a modern economy by the year 2015.

Food security - The emphasis is on the development of modern technology, research, financial injection into research, production and development of agricultural inputs leading to a 5 to 10-fold increase in yields and production. This is supposed to result in massive domestic and commercial output and technological knowledge transfer to farmers.

Wealth creation - This reform is focused on wealth creation through diversified production especially in the agricultural and solid mineral sector. This requires Nigerians to "choose" to work, as hard work by all is required to achieve this reform.

Transport sector - The transportation sector in Nigeria with its poor road networks is an inefficient means of mass transit of people and goods. With the goal of a modernized and industrialized Nigeria, it is mandatory that Nigeria develop its transport sector.

Land reforms - While hundreds of billions of dollars have been lost through unused government-owned landed assets, changes in the land laws and the emergence of land reforms is supposed to optimise Nigeria's growth through the release of land for commercialised farming and other large-scale business by the private sector. The result is supposed to assure improvements and boosts to the production and "wealth creation initiatives".

Security - An unfriendly security climate apparently "precludes both external and internal investment into the nation". Thus, security will be not only a constitutional requirement but also as a necessary infrastructure for the development of a "modern Nigerian economy". With its needs, the Niger Delta security issue will be the primary focus, marshalled not with physical policing or military security, but through "honest and accurate dialogue" between the people and the Federal Government.

Education - The two-fold reforms in the educational sector are supposed to achieve the "minimum acceptable international standards of education for all." With that achieved a strategic educational development plan "will ensure excellence in both the tutoring and learning of skills in science and technology" by students who will be the "future innovators and industrialists of Nigeria." This reform is to be achieved through massive injection into the Education sector.

## FAILURE OF PLAN

This plan did not achieve its set. Most of these reforms were not properly analysed and concrete plan put in place, power. The plan was to generate 10,000MW of electricity for a country with population of 140 million people as at the time the plan was reeled out, the country could not exceed 4,200MW, which is grossly inadequate. There was no clear-cut plan with respect to technology for the farmers to enable the 5-10-fold increase of food production.

**What our plans Look like (RECAST PLEASE)**

Having looked at various national plans immediately after independence and its ineffectiveness, the oil boom and excessive spending as well as the effects it had on the economy when oil stopped booming in 1981.

According to john Hackett, 'The development plan attempts to promote economic development in four main ways:

(1) By assessing the current state of the economy and providing information about it.

(2) By increasing the overall rate of investment;

(3) By carrying out special types of investment designed to break bottlenecks in production in important sectors of the economy.

(4) By trying to improve the coordination between different parts of the economy. Of these, the first and fourth are perhaps the most important and the least understood function of economic planning

The other two functions of planning cannot be efficiently carried out without ample and reliable information, nor without effective economic coordination between the different government departments and agencies within the public sector and the private sector. In most developing countries, information about the economy is scarce, and planning has provided the impetus to acquire and analyse the necessary data in order to provide a better understanding of the functioning of the economy. In order to improve coordination it is necessary to spread reliable economic information to indicate the future course of the government's economic intentions and activities so that the people concerned, both in the public and the private sectors, may make appropriate plans of their own to bring them in line with the government's plan.

It has been difficult to provide accurate data on the economy and this has been a challenge for the nation, most of the planning is done based on certain assumptions, there is no much data to analyse at the point of taking some decisions, and this is one of the factors responsible for the failure of most developmental plans in Nigeria. Coordination's between departments, government agencies; there are no handshake between this entities, this makes it difficult for an accurate planning to be done. The government should ensure this is achieved in the nearest future so as to ensure that the country is in the right direction with respect to economy planning. As a country mechanism should be put in place to handle data collection properly, eliminate errors as much as possible.

**Political Leadership** Voters determines who gets to the public office. This is in the ideal situation but reverse is the case of Nigeria as politicians rig elections or the population of the voters is poor compared to the exact population, the electoral body find it difficult to distribute the Permanent Voters' cards to the owners as well as old people taking up most political offices. The only way this can be checkmated this is to encourage the youths to participate actively in politics and serious and rigorous political reorientation.

Patriotism is one ingredient missing in the present crop of politicians one wonders why they care only about themselves, budgets are not passed in good time and this has a negative effect on the economy.

Nigerians needs to demand good governance , encourage law makers in the national Assembly to sponsor relevant bills that will improve standard of living in Nigeria. This should be done peacefully and within the provisions of the law.

**Education**

Quality education is the only way citizens can remain creative and contribute positively to economic advancement. Participation of the government and private sector the education of the citizens is very necessary. The government should fund education properly by allocating more resources to this sector, the so called 'Education disadvantage states' should be covered adequately by ensuring these communities are sensitized on the importance of sending their wards to school. Some years ago, the Federal Government embarked on a school feeding programme, the aim of the programme is to provide free lunch for pupils in government owned primary school. This is a good idea as it will help consolidate the achievement of the Goodluck Jonathan administration especially on the establishment of Almajiri Schools in northern Nigeria.

The Ministry of Education should be proactive on technical education in Nigeria, look at innovation that can be introduced that will add value to our society and create Jobs in both formal and informal sector of our economy.

Stress should be given to the importance of Polytechnic education to the development of the nation, Garba (WHICH GARBA? STATE HIS FULL NAME AND POSITION) said that the comprehensive policy on Polytechnic education was included in the National Policy on Education under set objectives on technical education which include: the provision of trained manpower in Applied Sciences, Technology and Commerce, particularly at sub-professional grades; the provision of the technical knowledge and vocational skills necessary for agricultural, industrial, commercial and economic development and the provision of people who can apply scientific knowledge to the improvement the solution of environmental problems for the use and convenience of mankind.

There is need to do more with respect to current trends which is obtainable internationally, technologies that would improve the services to be rendered should be encouraged.

The Private sector must learn to give back to the society, they can float vocational centres in rural areas, organise training that will boost food productions, banks should be involved, they are the ones that will dispense funds from CBN for anchor borrowers programs, providing trainings will ensure that the funds are adequately utilised and the goals for such disbursements are met. Professor Azaiki explained that another reason for the involvement of the private sector in education development, at any level in Nigeria, is "to deploy scarce funds to provide those basic infrastructure; learning aids, tools and equipment; qualified and well-informed cadre of teachers and instructors in the privately-owned institutions at the service of the community in the areas of functional instruction methods and purpose-driven total education of the Nigerian child".

## Security Challenges

Nigeria has experienced series of killings and other security challenges for some time now. USD2.6 billion was spent in 2016 fighting boko haram insurgency, converting this to naira, Nigeria have spent 936 billion naira. While there is need to acquire sophisticated military weapons, it is also important that the whole security architecture is reviewed.

Insecurity in Nigeria can be greatly reduced when the Vigilante Groups of Nigeria (that present in the 774 local government areas and the 36 states of the federation including the Federal Capital Territory, Abuja), the Nigerian

Police Force and other security agencies in the country is fully brought to function. The president as a matter of urgency needs to sign the Vigilante Group of Nigeria Bill into law as a way of legitimizing their duties. Security is everyone's responsibility and integrating the VGN into the present architecture will go a long way in complimenting the police. The present involvement of the military in internal security should be discouraged as the military should only be involved in defending the country's territorial integrity.

Local policing makes it easy for eradication of crime. For an example, civilian Joint Task Force (JTF) has over the years proved to be useful in the fight against insurgency in Borno State. They have been effective to a large extent and they is need to encourage their contributions.

Another reason to encourage the existence of local vigilante groups in Nigeria officers is that they live within the communities. This makes it easier for them to identify strange people and odd movements in their locality thereby utilising intelligence-led community policing that is proactive to curb crimes, instead of the reactive and reactionary policing system that is currently operational in Nigeria.

The current state of the Nigerian Police Force should be reviewed; the recruitment strategies, promotional policies as well as other welfare packages of police officers needs to be reviewed. This will go a long way in encouraging the officers.

## National Agriculture Programme

Agriculture remains a very important vocation all over the world; most countries earn foreign exchange from exports. This is one very area the government needs to look into. The current government is doing well in this regard. Intervention funds have been provided for Rice farms by the Federal Government. There is need for this initiative to be extended to other food and cash crops in the country.

Nigeria is the largest producer of cassava in the world. West Africa produces 20 percent of world cassava consumptions annually. Although Nigeria has an enormous market for cassava production, it is mostly grown for family consumption and local sale by smallholders. This field faces many challenges because of the use outdated technology as well inadequate storage facilities for the product. These challenges over the years caused low productivity and postharvest losses.

Nigeria cannot afford to give-up on reviving Agriculture. Agriculture if harnessed very well has the ability to revive the economy, create jobs, boost productions of crops for exports. Cassava for instance, when processed can be useful in the production of ethanol.

Ethanol is presently produced from molasses in several countries, but cassava, a starch- accumulating tuber crop with up to 30% of fermentable, appears to hold more benefits when used for industrial ethanol production. Sukphisal, a seasoned writer in 2005 reported that the total output for cassava ethanol was projected to reach about 3.4 million litres per day in Thailand. This study is in agreement with what Atthasampunna stated earlier in 1987 when he noted that while the basic procedures for obtaining ethanol from cassava have been well defined, there is need to improve on technologies relating to efficiency and increased yields when compared to other substrates.

As a nation, there is need to take advantage of this plant and earn foreign exchange from export and also take care of local consumption. Technology should be provided with respect to food production, farmers should be trained on the use of machines like tractors, irrigation farming, food preservation etc. The Federal Ministry of Agriculture in conjunction with the state ministries and other stakeholders organise trainings in the various local governments. This is to teach the local farming population how to make use of the technologies to be provided. Programme should be developed to encourage people to embark on agriculture for commercial purposes. This is a way of been self-reliant in food production and impact positively on the economy. A classic example is cassava production. Its production would enable Nigeria meet local demand and maintain her position as one of the world's largest producer.

There is need to review performance of food production and take proactive steps for improvements, this will be very beneficial as issues will be identified and solutions prescribed. It will also have a bottom line effect on all the sectors of the economy. As a nation there is need to pursue an Agro-economy, the United States for an instance has recorded huge success in this area despite have other area of expertise. Agricultural sector unemployment rate is dropping at a faster rate than the rest of the job specialties this is as a result of what Vilsack in the Agriculturist Newspaper calls "an extraordinary investment in infrastructure." He describes it as an extensive supply chain including storage, transport, and equipment manufacturing.

According to him, Farmers are buying lots of new machinery, like large tractors with sophisticated GPS systems as well as other new farming technologies. This has led to new hiring on the part of companies like John Deere, which recently added 250 people at a plant in Iowa, United States of America that manufactures cotton pickers.

The private and public sector is encouraged to embark on "back to farm" programme, this programme should aim at encouraging people to take of farming as an alternative job. There is also need to provide facilities and encouragements that will enable these workers take the vocation seriously. This will help to create employment; though an informal sector and such jobs hitherto were seasonal can be all round with the advent of irrigational technologies.

**Unemployment Challenge**

The National Bureau of Statistics (NBS) in a report released late last year stated in its Labour Force Statistics that the unemployment rate in

Nigeria is 23.1%; an increase of 3% compared to the figures of 2017 which was 18.1%.
There is need for this to be addressed urgently. This is to be reduced or eliminated. There have been series of attempts to tackle this problem by the present government at state and federal levels. These programmes are not yielding the right result and there is need for the review of the actions being taken. The government needs to show more political will power in tackling the challenge. Nigeria needs to borrow a leaf from the Chinese economy. The Chinese economy has 95% of its gross Domestic Product (GDP) based on Small and medium Scale Enterprise. Their strategy is to produce world's needs from funding are given by financial institutions with favourable rate. Nigerians needs to be creative, turn their passion into wealth, research into areas that are viable to world economy and start up something in that regard.

There is need to encourage the unemployed youths to become entrepreneurs, provide empowerment programmes. This could take different shape; The Tony Elumelu Foundation for an example requests for business proposals from young people to be sent and reviewed. If approved, the candidate is invited to attend series of seminars which involves successful entrepreneurs and afterwards a grant is disbursed. This initiative has being able to empower thousands of people and more of such programmes needs to be established by both the public and private sector.

The best strategy for Nigeria as a nation to tackle unemployment is to adopt the Chinese model. One question that pops up is the state of the infrastructure in Nigeria. Can it support this initiative? Hope must not be given up in this regard. It is on records that the cost of production in Nigeria is very high and this definitely impact on price of these products. The government need to improve the ease of doing business and develop industrial parks nationwide, where state of the art infrastructure can be developed to aid industrial revolution and ease the high cost of production.

## Role of Religious Leaders

Religious leaders need to do more in educating their followers. Social vices like suicide are on the rise in the country. The rate of suicide in the country is on the rise. This rise is as a result of challenges of failed business, inability to meet financial obligations, difficult economic conditions, academic challenges and others.
Religious Leaders should teach their followers values that will help them to understand the value of patience, perseverance, as well as the dignity of labour. Most importantly, they should help these affected financially to meet their need and see how they can support them to come out the present problem by offering an important advise.

Today religious Leaders in Nigeria are not living up to expectation; they are only interested in collecting contributions from the people instead of them to support efforts being put in place to eradicate poverty. They should preach peace, unity and patriotism to their congregation, advice against corruption and other negative vices in our society.

The role of our religious leaders is so vital in nation building when it comes to morals and behavioural patterns in the lives of their followers, this will rub on our nation positively.

Also religious Leaders they should tell the government of the day the truth with respect to their performance and ensure it's improved rather than deceive them. Teach your followers the truth about life, most importantly essence of sacrifice, living a good life, Fear of God, trust and believe in God. There is no religion that does not talk about these things I have mentioned in this paragraph, we need to build our followers so that they will remain on track with the Almighty God.

## Commercial banks involvement

Commercial banks in Nigeria should be involved in nation building, I quite commend their efforts in cooperate social responsibilities nationwide and supporting central bank in conducting trainings for SME's and intervention funds disbursements and also funding SME's to an extent and with respect to our discussions about unemployment.

The banks can be proactive by selling products that can have an impact on Nigeria economy positively. I'm quite sure the question is already ringing in our minds ***'how can this happen?'*** the products will be hinged on agriculture, The bank can lease Agriculture implements, processing machines for rice, Garri and other relevant machineries to farmers and the clause in the arrangement should be that these machineries should be deployed in the rural areas that are predominantly farmers that will use the infrastructure to process their produce for a fee, what have been achieved is that the pains experienced by our farmers have been eased and the investor receives a fee and bank facility maintained.

One of Nigeria major banks partnered with DBN, they accessed 25 billion naira that will be disbursed to SME's, wonderful initiatives that will help lift up the economy positively and other banks to take a cue from this.

We cannot blame our banks, mitigating the associated risks involved in Lending is a major factor restraining them from these initiatives, nevertheless they should not drop the ball but look for how to walk through such challenges, the bottom line is that they must remain in business.

Nigeria banks should also play roles in creating empowerment programmes in the rural areas of Federation, this will help in alleviating poverty and this should be done in conjunction with the state government and this is yielding positive results. Development banks are doing a lot in this direction and I want to encourage them to make adequate funds available for those that need them and ensure its properly deployed, this is where follow up with these SME's are very important and this should not be neglected in anyway.

# Chapter 7

## The crux of the matter

Personally, I want to commend the efforts of the President Muhamadu Buhari's administration in fighting corruption but there's need for agencies involved not to operate like robots, rather should sought proactive steps to tackle this virus that has eaten deep into our fabric since independence until now.

It is noteworthy that Singapore used to be a very corrupt nation but today this issue has been tackled and it's advisable we study their model, with little modification and adoption. With this, I believe we will surely get to the promise land. We need to be patriotic as a Citizens of Nigeria and exhibit the love for our nation; this will make us want to do anything for our nation. Let us borrow a leaf from Abraham Lincoln, Let us think of what we can do for Nigeria and not what Nigeria can do for us', Nigeria is our nation, there is nowhere like home and we need ensure we are united as a single entity and put in our best with regards nation building.

As a nation Nigeria is involved in a lot of waste are engaged in waste of resources i.e. security votes, Constituency allowance, Cost of governance etc., I want to use this medium to advise that these wastages should be eliminated and deployed to other parts of our economy. Security votes is often abused and must be discontinued, let's look at some figures below;

| SECURITY VOTES | |
|---|---|
| STATE | AMOUNT RCVD =N= |
| ABIA | 8,400,000,000 |
| ADAMAWA | |
| AKWA IBOM | 21,600,000,000.00 |
| ANAMBRA | 10,000,000,000.00 |
| BAUCHI | 17,000,000,000.00 |
| BAYELSA | |
| BENUE | 37,100,000,000.00 |
| BORNO | 9,675,000,000.00 |
| CROSS RIVER | 6,000,000,000.00 |
| DELTA | 24,000,000,000.00 |
| EBONYI | |
| EDO | 10,800,000,000.00 |
| EKITI | 1,200,000,000.00 |
| ENUGU | 7,200,000,000.00 |
| IMO | 4,000,000,000.00 |
| KADUNA | 4,800,000,000.00 |
| KANO | 0 |
| KATSINA | 211,000,000.00 |
| KOGI | 4,800,000,000.00 |
| KWARA | 0 |
| LAGOS | 17,149,000,000.00 |
| NASSARAWA | 1,200,000,000.00 |
| NIGER | 15,700,000,000.00 |
| OGUN | 1,200,000,000.00 |
| ONDO | 7,200,000,000.00 |
| OSUN | 4,800,000,000.00 |
| OYO | |
| PLATEAU | 2,600,000,000.00 |
| RIVERS | 18,000,000,000.00 |
| SOKOTO | 0 |
| TARABA | 2,400,000,000.00 |
| YOBE | 3,800,000,000.00 |
| ZAMFARA | 7,200,000,000.00 |
| | |
| | |
| | |
| | 248,035,000,000 |

This indicates that Nigeria spends 248.035 billion annually on security votes in Nigeria, what a waste of resources. These monies cannot be accounted for and should be put to a stop. These resources can be can be deployed to other initiatives that will boost our economy, releasing these funds means that we are encouraging corruption.

Let us look at the resource allocated to our law makers for constituency zonal intervention project; 100 billion is allocated annually for this purpose of carrying out projects in their communities. In recent years, the budget of the Zonal Intervention Projects has been N100 billion shared among the 469 senators and members of the House of Representatives in the six geo-political zones. Specific details on the projects, including project type, cost, and target sector have been kept secret in the past because lawmakers engage in self-enriching deals in the implementation of the projects. Thus constituents hardly know what should statutorily accrue to them.

Implementing the zonal intervention projects does not involve cash payments or any other form of payment to a legislator. The duties of the legislator are simply to identify the location and the type of project to be sited. Once this is done, it will be included in the budget of the relevant MDA by the National Assembly. Even though the projects are advertised in line with the Public Procurement Act, only contractors nominated by the lawmakers are often awarded the contracts. At times some lawmakers nominate companies in which they have interests.

In some cases, contractors awarded jobs only move the cash to lawmakers who nominated them and the contracts are not implemented in some instances.

This is another waste, these funds flows into the pocket of the lawmakers, it's the reason why law makers struggle to get to the chambers, during electoral process they perpetuate tactics to win elections, the chambers have become a platform for governors that have completed 2 terms, they proceed there and also enjoy the largesse. How can we develop if we continue to waste resources, in my candid opinion this arrangement should be discontinued, the constituencies are not in any way developed, this is an approved waste of public funds.

Despite the fact that there are framework for ensuring the funds get to the constituents , trust a corrupt mind they have a way of beating the system and diverting funds via the contractors or they use their companies to execute this contract.

These two (2) heads are part of cost of governance, how many government aids should be employed by these politicians, there is no limit, most times they want to satisfy party fateful and the list grows and there are no standards.

There was a time the former governor of Central Bank of Nigeria and now Emir of Kano, Alhaji Muhammadu Sanusi II called for a reduction in the cost of governance in the country with a warning that about 70 per cent of the federal government's revenue goes into the payment of salaries and entitlements, leaving 30 per cent for development.

It is pertinent to emphasise that a lean government will reduce waste, inefficiency, corruption and duplication of government functions as well as make capital spending more effective. Dysfunctional at best, the Nigerian economy is groaning under the weight of excessive cost of governance. Essentially, a huge portion of the country's resources is allocated to servicing a tiny fraction of the population who are public office holders. With little left for the provision of social infrastructure, the majority is entrenched in extreme poverty, which is why the acting Chairman of the Revenue Mobilisation, Allocation and Fiscal Commission, Shettima Abba-Gana, has canvassed a methodical reduction in the cost of governance.

After serving out their tenure, governors obnoxiously receive mega pensions – for life. About four years ago, a state awarded N200 million in annual pension to each of its ex-governors. It is laughable because these governors served their states for just eight years – or less. It is daylight robbery of the public still.

Ludicrously, these governors earned top rates while in office and used chartered/private jets, although their citizens live in penury. In contrast, the British Prime Minister and Queen Elizabeth II travel in commercial aircraft for her assignments.

Cost of governance is a major disconnect with respect to Nigeria's development, recurrent expenditure accounts for 70% and the balance is grossly inadequate for our development of infrastructure. the error is been made by past administration, the agency given this responsibility of RMAFC (STATE THE FULL MEANING), there's little they can accomplish as the constitution remains the guide and it's important for us to note that the 1999 constitution must be amended to correct these issues once and for all.

The idea of State governors in Nigeria being paid pensions after ruling for just 8 years should be abolished, rich states even go as far as building a retirement house for these former chief executives, when are we going to stop all these wastes, I'm not against remuneration for past leaders but it should be reasonable, even our past head of states are part of these arrangement. I just want to encourage that we take positive steps in addressing this challenge facing our nation, holding political office has turned to meal ticket and not service to the nation, most times they pretend that the interest of our nation is the utmost priority. No lawmaker can sponsor any bill that will address the high cost of governance; there is need to start with parastatals agencies whose functions are duplicated. Below are some examples:

- Economic and Financial Crimes' Commission (EFCC) and Independent Corrupt Practices Commission ( ICPC).
- The Nigerian Police Force (NPF) and Federal Road Safety Corps (FRSC).
- Nigerian Ports Authority (NPA), Nigerian Maritime Administration and Safety Agency (NIMASA), National Inland Waterways Authority (NIWA)

- National Information Technology Development Agency (NITDA) and Nigeria Communications Satellite Limited (NIGCOMSAT)
- Bureau of Public Enterprises (BPE) and Bureau of Public Procurement (BPP)
- Nigeria Investment Promotion Commission (NIPC), Nigerian Export - Import Bank (NEXIM Bank), Nigerian Export Promotion Council (NEPC) and Nigeria Export Processing Zones Authority (NEPZA).
- National Teachers Institute (NTI) and Teachers Registration Council of Nigeria (TRCN).
- Electricity Management Services Limited (EMSL), Energy Commission of Nigeria (ECN) , National Power Training Institute of Nigeria (NAPTIN), Nigerian Electricity Regulatory Commission (NERC) and Rural Electrification Agency (REA).
- National Biosafety Management Agency (NBMA), National Environmental Standards and Regulations Enforcement Agency

(NESREA) and National Oil Spill Detection and Response Agency (NOSDRA).

- Defence Intelligence Agency (DIA), Department Security Service (DSS) and National Intelligence Agency (NIA).
- National Judicial Council (NJC) and Federal Judicial Service Commission (FJSC)
- Broadcasting Organisation of Nigeria (BON) and News Agency of Nigeria (NAN)
- National Biotechnology Development Agency (NABDA) and National Centre for Remote Sensing, Jos (NCRS).
- Nigeria Hydrological Services Agency (NIHSA) , Nigerian Integrated Water Resources Commission , National Water Resources Institute (NWRI) and River Basin Development Authorities (RBDA's)
- National Salaries, Incomes and Wages Commission (NSIWC) and (STATE FULL MEANING) RMAFC

These listed agencies has overlapping functions, it make more economy sense to merge them for better efficiency and reduce cost of funding, various administrations established these Agencies to address some pressing national issues, this will eliminate the waste & reduce recurrent expenditures, we need to build strong institutions that will add value to our country by been very effective and not redundant.

Nigerians also needs to reduce their taste for foreign goods. The implication of this quest for foreign goods is that Nigeria enriches other countries. Despite the fact that Nigerian customs Service has placed ban on the importation of some goods, these products still gets to the country because of the porous nature of the Nigerian borders. This anomaly has a negative effect on the economy as it makes it difficult for local enterprise to strive.

With this enormous challenge, the question begs that begs for an answer is that why do most people prefer foreign-made to Nigerian made?

While it cannot be argued that most buy foreign-made just to show off their elite status, there are other reasons that stare at us in the eye. The most common is the way and manner most Nigerian goods are produced. The production process and packaging are sometimes defective and uncreative.

Local firms should live up to expectations by improving the quality of their products to match with international standards. This can be achieved with better focus on Research & development in these industries.

Medical tourism is another source of leakage with respect to foreign exchange, according to the immediate past Minister of State for Health, Dr Osagie Ehanire, Nigeria spends over $1bn annually on medical treatment. The question is if the people can be blamed for this anomaly.

Health facilities in the country is in a deplorable are condition, Health workers always on strike and other challenges facing the health sector. There is need for an upgrade and improvement on the infrastructure and acquire the state of the art equipments in the hospitals. The welfare package of the health workers needs to be improved upon. This is to reduce the rate of recurrent strike actions and also reduce the recent migration of Nigerian health workers to other countries in search of greener pastures

The culture of Nigerians preferring anything foreign is also a contributory factor to the mass exodus of Nigerians for medical treatment abroad. According to a study by Bruce (2016), Nigerians have insatiable appetite for anything foreign.

***(In September 2015, the General Assembly of UN adopted the 2030 Agenda for Sustainable Development that includes 17 Sustainable Development Goals (SDGs). Building on the principle of "leaving no one behind", the new Agenda emphasizes a holistic approach to achieving sustainable development for all. The Goal 3: Ensure healthy lives and promote well-being for all at all ages The Target 3.6 under goal 3 is designed specifically to addresses the issue of road traffic accident: By 2020, halve the***

***number of global deaths and injuries from road traffic accidents.***

We have not look at sports, it's the greatest sector creating jobs for our youths in Nigeria, good enough Football is given more attention than other sports, good enough private sector is also involved in sports development via sponsorships and I believe they can do more in this direction. The state our facilities like stadiums are in deplorable condition, can we remember the national stadium, Surulere hosted nations cup in 1980 , 2002 and various world cup qualifying matches , today it's in a very bad state due to lack of maintenance.

Great sports icons have been produced in Nigeria and I believe we can achieve more with good administration, funding and provision of quality infrastructure, exposure of our athletes to foreign competitions, tournaments etc. , great talents are abound.

## Conclusion

Nigeria can be great, she is blessed with natural resources, human capital that has proved to be among the best in the world. Nation building is a collective responsibility of the citizenry, government other stake holders.

Nigeria's democracy is still evolving has witnessed an uninterrupted democracy since 1999. Nigerians needs to exhibit patriotism, dignity of labour, hard work, perseverance, shun violence when pressing for demands and peacefully achievements can be recorded.

There is a wind of revolution is blowing across Africa and Nigeria cannot be left out. Nigerians needs to shun corrupt elements in all entirety and expose anyone found wanting.

It is the belief of this author that the security challenges in the country will be fixed soon. Nigerians however needs to furnish the security operatives with timely information to assist them in their fight against crime.

## References

Amodu, B. (2018) Nigeria Records Reduced Rice Import. Leadership Newspaper. November 7, 2018

Ewubare, K. (2017) *Former Minister blames Obasanjo for Nigeria's economic woes.* Thisday Newspaper , November 3, 2017

Natre, B.R (2016), Journal, *Groundnut pyramid in Nigeria: can they be revived?*, ICRISAT Bamako.

Umezulike, C (2017) *A reflection on the legacies of muritala Mohammed.* Code Journal

, Dr Bonny R. Natre(2017), British Colonial policies and oil palm industry in the Niger Delta , ICRISAT Journal

Malaysia never took palm seed from Nigeria, Vanguard 13th Sept 2013., Adefaye A.

Malaysia palm oil industry, Journal of oil palm, environment & health

List of mineral resources in Nigeria, information Guide in Nigeria.

How Sweden created a model economy, Sweden Sverige , 2018

## About the Author

Alex Ndukwe holds a Post graduate diploma in Theology from Redeemed Christian Bible College; a graduate of School of Disciples.

He also holds a degree in computer science from University of Nigeria Nsukka, A master's Degree in business administration from Ambrose Alli University Ekpoma and Doctorate degree in computer science, Atlantic international University, Florida, USA.

Dr. Ndukwe also holds various ICT certifications including ISO 20000, COBIT 5, ITIL v3 certifications etc.

He is an experienced information technology expert with experience spanning over 22 years managing ICT infrastructure in the banking industry. He previously worked with Indo-Nigerian bank Limited and Sterling Bank Plc.

Currently, he is the the Chief Executive Officer (CEO), Tekville Systems, an ICT consulting firm based at Abuja and also a Part-time pastor with the One-Accord Gospel Church

He is married to Mrs. Ada Ndukwe and their marriage is blessed with 3 children: Deborah, David & Daniel.

www.ingramcontent.com/pod-product-compliance
Lightning Source LLC
Chambersburg PA
CBHW032113280326
41933CB00009B/823

*9780359831685*